TRANSATLANTIC LINERS

J. Kent Layton

SHIRE PUBLICATIONS

Published in Great Britain in 2012 by Shire Publications Ltd, Midland House, West Way, Botley, Oxford OX2 0PH, United Kingdom.

44-02 23rd Street, Suite 219, Long Island City, NY 11101, USA.

E-mail: shire@shirebooks.co.uk   www.shirebooks.co.uk

A CIP catalogue record for this book is available from the British Library.

Shire Library no. 660.   ISBN-13: 978 0 74781 087 2

J. Kent Layton has asserted his right under the Copyright, Designs and Patents Act, 1988, to be identified as the author of this book.

Designed by Tony Truscott Designs, Sussex, UK and typeset in Perpetua and Gill Sans.

Printed in China through Worldprint Ltd.

12 13 14 15 16   10 9 8 7 6 5 4 3 2 1

COVER IMAGE
A painting commissioned by Cunard for the *Queen Mary 2*, showing the *Mauretania* outbound from Liverpool. (Courtesy of Cunard, with special thanks to GB Marine Art.)

TITLE PAGE IMAGE
Laid up in Long Beach, California, the *Queen Mary* is a reminder of the glory days of the transatlantic liners. This view looks from her forecastle towards the superstructure.

CONTENTS PAGE IMAGE
A splendid cutaway view of the *United States* in period publicity material.

ACKNOWLEDGEMENTS
I would like to thank my friends and family for encouraging me to pursue a career in maritime history and to those who have contributed to my research over the years. Also particular thanks go to those who have contributed or allowed me to use illustrations for this publication, which are acknowledged as follows (referenced to page numbers):

Brown Brothers: 23; Corbis Images: 46, 49 (top), 55 (bottom); Dave Evans: 59; Ioannis Georgiou Collection: 12, 14 (bottom left), 36 (top); John Hudson: 58; Imperial War Museum: 29; Library of Congress, Prints & Photographs Division: 18 (top), 31 (bottom), 35, 36 (bottom); J&C McCutcheon Collection: 43 (top), 44 (bottom), 45, 49 (bottom), 57; Marc & Karen Pierson: 1, 60 (top), 61 (top); Mike Poirier Collection: 9, 10 (top), 11, 16 (bottom left), 28 (top), 34 (bottom), 48, 55 (top), 62; Richard Smye Collection: 28 (bottom); Courtesy of the White Swan Hotel: 18 (bottom).

All remaining images are from the author's collection.

Shire Publications is supporting the Woodland Trust, the UK's leading woodland conservation charity, by funding the dedication of trees.

CONTENTS

WHITE STAR LINE

R.M.S. "Oceanic" 704 feet long, 17.274 ton
Services to New York, South Africa,
          Australia and New Zealand.
Ismay, Imrie & Co. London & Liverpool.

THE EMERGENCE OF THE SUPERLINER

A S THE NINETEENTH CENTURY was drawing to a close, incredible progress
had been made in the design of seagoing vessels. As that century began,
ships were wooden-hulled, sail-powered craft ranging from less than a
hundred tons up to several thousand tons for prestigious naval 'ships of the
line'. The speed and safety of the passage across the ocean depended greatly
on prevailing winds for propulsion, and many of these craft were lost when
the capricious whims of nature turned violent. Schedules were difficult to
keep – particularly when ships came upon doldrums. If navigators became
uncertain of their location, or made even minor errors in judgement at
critical moments when in the vicinity of the shore, disaster was often not
far off. This was particularly true when sailing vessels found themselves too
close to dangerous shorelines with the winds against them. Indeed, many
vessels merrily set sail from port with cargo and passengers, and were never
seen or heard of again.

As the industrial revolution began to take firm hold on land, however, it was
only natural to expect that keen minds would begin to apply technology to the
problems of ocean travel, and this they did. The application of steam engines
and of iron, and then steel, hulls allowed ships both to abandon reliance on
sails and to offer unprecedented comforts to prospective passengers. Ships
grew larger and faster with astonishing speed, and competition on the North
Atlantic – which connected Europe and the Americas, and was thus a focal
point for international trade between the world's leading powers – grew ever
greater. There was also no small amount of national pride over who had the
world's largest, fastest or most luxurious ocean liners, and this further drove
competition between the great steamship lines.

Despite the hazards involved, there were many reasons why people
travelled across the Atlantic. Some travelled for business, some for pleasure,
and others formed part of the mass migration from the Old World to the
New. These passengers were divided into different categories, or classes,
based on their financial and social status. Immigrants formed a large
proportion of ocean-going clientele. Steamship lines provided them with

Opposite:
An advertisement
for the White Star
liner *Oceanic* of
1899, showing her
fine lines and
proud funnels.

simple, relatively inexpensive accommodation in the less desirable areas of their ships, and found great profits in doing so. This group comprised third class, also known as steerage in a term held over from the early days of immigrant ships. In some continental vessels, third class was subdivided again to form third class and fourth class/steerage.

Above was second class, where one found business people, teachers, students, and other middle-class people. Their accommodation was comfortable, spacious, and well thought out. First-class passenger lists, by way of comparison, included very successful businessmen, stars of the stage, heads of state and royalty, and the stratospherically wealthy. They were given the most desirable locations on the ship, and no expense was spared in giving them the most comfortable and luxurious accommodation.

Passengers in general were keen to travel on the largest, fastest and most prestigious ships. In the name of technological progress, sails had eventually given way to steam engines with screw propellers, wooden hulls to iron and then to steel, and clipper stems to knife-like vertical prows. Ships became more reliable, and were better able to withstand the navigational hazards and forces of nature that they encountered. Taking passage across the Atlantic had become less of an overtly danger-fraught ordeal and more of a routine occurrence.

Then on 14 January 1899, the next great step forward in maritime progress took to the water for the first time. Built for the White Star Line – White Star and the Cunard Line held prominence as the two foremost British steamship companies – this great vessel was named *Oceanic*. The launch ceremonies took place in the prominent Harland & Wolff shipyard, located in Belfast, Ireland. The *Oceanic*, actually the second ship of that name built for White Star, was the largest ship in the world at the time, at 704 feet in length and with a gross tonnage – a technical term that actually measured enclosed space rather than weight – of 17,272. She could carry over two thousand passengers and crew, and upon her maiden voyage in September 1899 from Liverpool to New York, she carried a near-capacity load of human cargo: 1,890. At a designed speed of 19 knots, the *Oceanic* was also a rather quick liner for her time. However, she was by no means a contender for the famous Blue Riband, the title held by any liner making a record-speed passage across the Atlantic. Yet the *Oceanic*'s unprecedented luxuries stunned the world. Her first-class interior appointments were described as being 'on a scale of magnificence made possible only by her size'. Indeed, one person who toured the ship just after her maiden voyage to New York was heard to remark that her steerage spaces were better than first-class spaces on ships just a few years before. Such unprecedented *luxe* made the *Oceanic* a tremendously valuable addition to White Star's fleet.

At the time of the *Oceanic*'s maiden voyage, the real groundbreaking speed-queens of the Atlantic were in the service of German steamship companies Norddeutscher Lloyd and Hamburg-Amerika. German dominance in the shipping industry's prestigious 'largest' and 'fastest' divisions was a rather recent development. Previously this title had been held by the British merchant marine, but Kaiser Wilhelm II of Germany wanted to see British supremacy challenged on every front, and backed the two German lines in their development of a new breed of technologically advanced superships. First to shock the world was the *Kaiser Wilhelm der Grosse* in 1897. She was followed by a number of other liners during succeeding years, including the *Deutschland* of 1900, and the *Kaiser Wilhelm II* of 1903. They were large and fast ships, happily holding the Blue Riband speed record among them for a full decade.

They also sported a unique profile. While most ships had one or two smokestacks, the German liners emerged from the shipyards with four proud, elegantly raked funnels. They were grouped in two natty-looking pairs; the next round of British contenders would copy the number of funnels, but preferred to stand them more or less evenly. Not everything about the German ships was positive, however; there were some justifiable sentiments expressed to the effect that their first-class spaces were rather ridiculously ostentatious, to a point clearly beyond good taste.

A postcard view of Hamburg-Amerika's *Deutschland*. This particular card was sent on 7 September 1901 by one of *Deutschland*'s passengers.

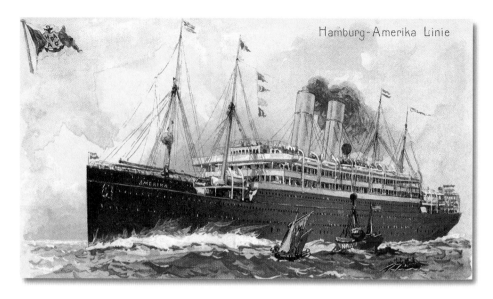

Hamburg-Amerika Linie

A splendid art postcard of the *Amerika* of 1905. While she looked traditional externally, her interior appointments were a bold step forward.

Additionally, there were times when these ships sacrificed passenger comfort for speed – as was the case with the *Deutschland* of 1900, a ship that still holds the notorious reputation of shaking its passengers near-senseless.

White Star countered the German display of speed by constructing a series of four giant liners which completely eschewed speed in favour of size and luxury. Each of these ships – named *Celtic* (1901), *Cedric* (1903), *Baltic* (1904) and *Adriatic* (1907) – was successively the largest vessel in the world, ranging from 20,904 up to 24,541 tons. Although quite comfortable, these four ships proved to be nearly impossibly slow, achieving speeds of 14–17 knots compared with the 22–3-knot averages being turned in by the new crop of German liners. Yet they were still the greatest ships in the world, and proved that speed was not the only ingredient in the recipe for a successful ship.

The Germans followed this trend with the advent of more comfortable liners like the *Amerika* of 1905. Built by Harland & Wolff of Belfast, the same yard which produced all new White Star tonnage – including the *Oceanic* (1899) and each of the 'Big Four' – the *Amerika* was a fantastic ship. While not as fast as other recent German liners, she was built very much like White Star's quartet of monster liners, albeit with an improved scheme of interior décor and finesse. She even boasted the first passenger elevator installed on an ocean liner.

In 1902, the White Star Line had been bought out by American financier J. P. Morgan, who was buying up numerous steamship lines and rolling them up together under the conglomerate banner of the International Mercantile Marine Group, or IMM. British mercantile pride had already been sorely

This view gives some idea of the finery of *Amerika's* first-class interior spaces. Finely dressed ladies and gentlemen make their *grande descente* to dinner in their finest formal attire.

bruised by the German contenders; this new development, although primarily a paper transfer that had little immediate effect on day-to-day operations, came as yet another blow to British prestige.

The Cunard Line – the sole remaining primary defender of Britain's maritime dominance on the Atlantic – was itself in a greatly inferior and steadily deteriorating position, when compared to White Star and the German lines. Cunard's last record-breaking vessels had been the *Campania* and *Lucania*, both dating to 1893 and being of less than 13,000 tons each. They were outsized and outpowered by their competitors.

On the other hand, Cunard did have a selection of nice intermediate vessels which served on the company's secondary routes. Foremost among these were the *Ivernia* (1899), *Saxonia* (1900) and *Carpathia* (1903). Each of these vessels was of about 13,000–14,000 tons, and they were built to similar specifications as a class of sister ships, even though they were built by two separate shipyards – the Scottish shipyard of John Brown & Company on the River Clyde, and the English yard of C. S. Swan & Hunter on the River Tyne. At a service speed of 14–15 knots, they would carry large amounts of cargo and nearly two thousand passengers each, most of those in steerage. These three ships were

A pair of first-class passengers engage in games on the boat deck of Cunard's *Ivernia*. From the way everyone is standing, the ship is clearly rolling.

Cunard's *Saxonia* pounding through heavy seas. Rough weather on the Atlantic was the norm rather than the exception.

tremendously successful in their intended role, but they certainly were not the prestigious ships needed to restore English supremacy on the Atlantic.

As early as 1901, Cunard began to investigate the possibility of building a pair of new superliners to take back the titles of 'world's largest' and 'world's fastest' ships. However, it was clear that Cunard simply could not

come up with the revenue to build the ships alone. Eventually, the company managed to secure financial backing for the venture from the British Government, and they began to proceed in earnest with their plans.

Although the next two Cunarders were to be a logical step in the evolution of Atlantic liners, they would, in retrospect, mark the true arrival of the 'superliner' on the North Atlantic.

Menu.

R. M. S. "CARPATHIA"

Sunday, July 17th., 1904.

-:DINNER:-

Caviare on Toast

Potage Chesterfield —:-:— Croute-au-Pot

Kenebec Salmon—Parsley Sauce—Cucumber

Ox Tail au Gratin —— Salmi of Duckling

Roast Spring Lamb—Mint Sauce

Calves' Head Vinaigrette Roast Turkey—Cranberry Sauce

Green Peas Cauliflower—Cream Sauce Boiled Rice

Boiled & Creamed Potatoes

Baked Cumberland Ham—Sauce Madeira

Shredded Lettuce

Plum Pudding—Sweet Sauce Apple Tart Sago Pudding

Mont Blanc Jelly Lemon Cheese Cakes

Sardine Butter on Toast

Neapolitan Ice Cream

Dessert

Crackers -:- Cheese -:- Coffee

This dinner menu from Cunard's *Carpathia* bears artwork featuring either the *Campania* or *Lucania*, legendary Cunarders from the early 1890s. Included among the ordering selections are such items as salmon, roast spring lamb with mint sauce, and roast turkey with cranberry sauce.

THE WONDER SHIPS

A NEW ERA in shipbuilding was dawning behind the scenes at the Cunard Company, and it was the beginning of a true golden age for the shipping industry. Their two proposed ships, eventually to be named *Lusitania* and *Mauretania*, were to be true wonders in every sense of the word. Their construction was contracted out to two different shipyards — *Lusitania* to the Scottish John Brown & Co., and *Mauretania* to the Tyneside Swan, Hunter & Wigham Richardson at Wallsend on Tyne. After two years of intense design study and refinement, the final blueprints for the two vessels suggested that they would be unprecedented marvels, but even that foregleam could not prepare the world for their finished forms, their physical presence. The *Lusitania* was laid down on 17 August 1904 and was launched on 7 June 1906. The *Mauretania*'s keel was laid down on 18 August 1904, and she was launched on 20 September 1906. *Lusitania* was some 787 feet in length, with a gross tonnage of 31,550; *Mauretania* was some 790 feet long, and was slightly larger at 31,937 tons.

At these dimensions, the two new ships were far and away the largest liners ever built. Their four smokestacks, slightly raked prows and counter sterns created an elegant and proud profile. Their interiors, afforded unprecedented space to work with, were nothing short of breathtaking; awed passengers on their first night aboard roamed the ships slack-jawed, enlisting the aid of stewards and stewardesses to find the dining saloons or the various public rooms, and even to get back to their own staterooms.

It was the ships' revolutionary powerplants, however, that really set them apart from every other crack Atlantic liner. To achieve an intended service speed of 25 knots, reciprocating engines — the tried-and-tested method of propelling all previous major liners — simply would not do. In June 1904, the decision was made to utilise a new propulsion technology, the marine steam turbine, to drive the new liners. Although turbines had never been used on this scale before, they would be the only way of achieving the required 68,000 horsepower required to realise the ships' intended service speed. It was a tremendous gamble, but it paid off in spades. When the *Lusitania*

Opposite:
This illustration of a dinner aboard Cunard's *Lusitania* conveys the splendour of the scene in a way that no black-and-white photo ever could.

A fine early view of the *Mauretania* in Liverpool.

entered service in September 1907, it was not long before she took the Blue Riband back to Britain; two months later, the *Mauretania* entered service, and took the trophy from her sister. During the next two years, the two enormous and immensely popular liners engaged in a friendly competition, passing the prize back and forth until, in September 1909, the *Mauretania*

Right: A scene during a typical crossing in the *Mauretania*'s first-class lounge and music room.

Far right: In this photo, dating from the summer of 1912, two officers pose with a pair of ladies from first class, on the sun deck astern of a funnel.

took the trophy for good. She was – by a very narrow margin – the faster of the two ships, and would hold the Blue Riband until 1929.

Though not as large or as fast as these Cunarders, two new ships were also being constructed by the Canadian Pacific Railway [CPR] company to run the Canadian route. Named *Empress of Britain* and *Empress of Ireland*, the twin-funnelled pair would enable passengers to travel – under the banner of a single company – from London to eastern Canada by steam, across Canada by rail, and thence by ship to Hong Kong. This was a remarkable offering at the beginning of the twentieth century. First to enter service was the *Empress of Britain*, of 14,189 tons, in May 1906. Her sister *Empress of Ireland*, slightly larger at 14,191 tons, entered service the following month. Each was 570 feet long, each was capable of transporting over 1,500 passengers, and both were built by the Fairfield Shipbuilding Company of Govan, Scotland. These two ships earned, over the next few years, a wonderful reputation for comfort and reliability.

Meanwhile, Harland & Wolff had constructed a liner named *Columbus* for the Dominion Line – a member of Morgan's conglomerate IMM – in 1903.

This late 1908 or early 1909 view of the *Lusitania* at her pier in New York shows her strength and proud form. The ship is re-coaling and preparing for her next east-bound crossing.

Canadian Pacific's *Empress of Ireland* of 1906. For eight years, she proved to be a comfortable and well-travelled vessel. She was paired up with her very similar sister, *Empress of Britain*, on the Canadian route to England.

Shipboard concerts, like this one held in third class aboard the *Empress of Ireland*, were usually held on the last or penultimate evening of a voyage to benefit seamen's charities. Talent usually came from non-professional passengers.

CANADIAN PACIFIC RAILWAY COMPANY

PROGRAMME OF CONCERT

IN AID OF THE
SEAMENS CHARITIES

R. M S. "EMPRESS OF IRELAND.

To be held in the Third Class

THURSDAY May 13th, 1909 at 8.0 p.m

CHAIRMAN   R. H WELDON, Esq

PART I

Song	Mr J Owens
Song	" True till Death " Mr G Hammond
Song	Mr A. Waddell
Song	H Shipley
Humorous Song	" T Bond
Song	Mr J W Smith
Humorous Song	H Tunstall

PART II

Song	Mr R. Dunk
Recitation	Miss Black
Song	Mr R Corrie
Humorous Song	H Tunsta l
Song	Mr S. Skossier
Song	H Shipley
Humorous Song	T Bond
Song	Mr H Whittaker

NATIONAL ANTHEMS

She was some 570 feet in length and measured 15,378 tons. Although roughly the same size as CPR's *Empresses*, she was designed to carry 2,830 passengers – some 2,300 of them in third class – in addition to her crew of about three hundred. After only two voyages with Dominion, she was transferred to IMM's flagship line, White Star, and renamed *Republic*. The single-funnel vessel was eventually placed on the New York–Mediterranean run. In the early morning hours of 23 January 1909, with over seven hundred passengers and crew aboard, the ship entered a thick fogbank off Nantucket. She was subsequently rammed by the Lloyd Italiano ship *Florida*. The collision killed three of *Republic*'s passengers and three of the *Florida*'s crew. The *Republic*'s engine and boiler rooms began to flood, and within minutes she had lost electrical power. Wireless distress calls – something of a novelty at the time – were sent out, and her passengers and crew were safely evacuated. The *Republic* sank the following day, the largest liner to founder on the Atlantic up to that time. She apparently took with her a large cargo of gold, perhaps up to three million dollars' worth in 1909 prices.

Republic's sinking was, rather ironically, touted as proof of the strength of modern ships and their safety. After all, she had sustained a cutting blow and had survived for a day after the impact; the only people killed were those who had perished in the actual collision. Finally, her CQD distress calls – CQ for 'All stations' and D for 'Distress' – had alerted nearby ships to her plight and had brought the required assistance. Public confidence in the safety of the Atlantic liners was unshaken.

White Star's *Republic*. Although of comparable size to the *Empress of Ireland*, she was designed to carry nearly eight hundred more passengers than the Canadian vessel. *Republic* sank after a collision in fog off Nantucket in 1909.

While these intermediate-sized ships were running various routes across the Atlantic, the main prestige still lay with the England to New York route. After 1907, the *Lusitania* and *Mauretania* certainly held the spotlight, but this did not last for long. Cunard's rival White Star began to move forward with plans to build their own pair of wonder ships for their crack service to New York. The plan was conceived by J. Bruce Ismay – head of the White Star Line, and son of the company's founder – and Lord William Pirrie, Chairman of Harland & Wolff shipyard. The formal order to proceed with plans for the ship was placed on 30 April 1907, and when the designs for the ships were finalised and approved, they would prove yet another quantum leap forward in liner design. White Star had long since eschewed any attempt on the Blue Riband, and had instead decided to focus on luxury. Because of this, their new liners would be half again as large as the Cunard fliers in interior volume. Their speed would be more moderate, and they would employ a combination of reciprocating engines and a single turbine powered from the exhaust of the two primary engines. Their intended service speed was 21 knots, but they would prove slightly faster. No matter what their speed, they would be without any doubt the most luxurious ships on the Atlantic. The first of these liners, *Olympic*, was laid down on 16 December 1908. The second ship – built directly alongside *Olympic* – was laid down on 31 March 1909. She was given the name *Titanic*.

Both liners were identical in length, at 882 feet 9 inches, and width. The *Olympic* was measured at some 45,324 tons, making her the largest vessel in the world. *Titanic* would be slightly larger at 46,329, due to some last-minute modifications to her passenger spaces. These latter alterations made for some visual differences between the two liners, but also gave *Titanic* bragging rights as 'world's largest ship' even if this was almost entirely an on-paper gain over her sister's measurement.

The story of the *Titanic* has really become the stuff of legend. However, up until *Titanic*'s tragic demise on her maiden voyage, it was really the *Olympic* that garnered the lion's share of the fame. *Olympic* was the first of the two great liners to be launched, and was given the undivided attention of both the public and press. Even on *Titanic*'s launch day, 31 May 1911, the *Olympic* still managed in many ways to steal the show. Freshly returned from successfully passing her two-day trials, and with her four buff black-topped funnels

gleaming brilliantly, the completed *Olympic* was boarded by some of the guests present for the launch of the *Titanic*, no doubt awed at her spaciousness and luxurious accommodations. *Olympic* departed Belfast that same afternoon bound for Liverpool, and thence proceeded to Southampton. Her maiden voyage to New York began on 14 June 1911, and was a very successful trip; within a short time she settled into her career, and enjoyed great popularity with the travelling public.

Over the remainder of that year and the beginning of 1912, the *Titanic* quietly inched closer to completion. This process was delayed by two mishaps with the *Olympic*. The first of these was quite serious, when she was involved in a collision with the cruiser HMS *Hawke*. The second was rather unremarkable, when she threw a propeller blade, and had to return to Belfast for a replacement. These two events, when combined, delayed *Titanic*'s completion to the point that her maiden voyage had to be postponed from 20 March to Wednesday 10 April 1912. Bookings for the crossing were also respectable, so much so that she would wind up carrying some 2,208

Just after noon on Wednesday 10 April 1912, *Titanic* cast off from her dock to begin a fateful and legendary crossing.

Although no colour photographs are known to exist of either *Olympic* or *Titanic*, this period illustration gives some sense of the scene as second-class passengers relax on the aft portion of one of the sisters' boat decks.

passengers and crew. Although she narrowly avoided a collision with another liner during her departure from Southampton that spring morning, the next few days of the crossing seemed quite routine. Many crewmembers from *Olympic* had transferred over to *Titanic*, including White Star's senior skipper, Captain Edward J. Smith. Smith's career was coming to a conclusion, as he had reached retirement age, and it seems that this round-trip voyage on the *Titanic* was to be his final command before dropping anchor permanently.

At this point, it is worth noting that both *Olympic* and *Titanic* were referred to as 'practically unsinkable', as one contemporary maritime journal said in 1911. White Star advertising for the sisters, dating to the late summer of 1910, stated that 'as far as it is possible to do so, these two wonderful vessels are designed to be unsinkable'. In the eyes of many, both ships were simply viewed as unsinkable. However, the *Olympic* and *Titanic* were not the only ships – before or since – that have been described thus. Indeed, in 1906, the Cunarders *Lusitania* and *Mauretania* had been called simply 'unsinkable', without any qualifying term. Captain Smith himself said in 1907, while Captain of the new *Adriatic*, that he could not 'imagine any condition which would cause a ship to founder. I cannot conceive of any vital disaster happening to this vessel. Modern shipbuilding has gone beyond that.' Confidence in the shipbuilding industry as a whole was so high that regulatory bodies like the British Board of Trade felt comfortable allowing big ships to take to the sea without providing lifeboat space for everyone aboard.

On Sunday 14 April 1912, the *Titanic* was steaming at over 22 knots. Numerous warnings of ice in her path had been received, but ice was to be expected in the vicinity at that time of year. The custom of the time was to proceed at full speed unless danger actually materialised. Confidence was placed in the officers and lookouts, as well as in the manoeuvrability of the ship, which was known to be quite good based on the data collected during her trials and those of the nearly identical *Olympic*. The weather was clear and visibility was excellent. Although much has been made, over the years, of the fact that the lookouts had no binoculars that night, the reality is that at the time binoculars were typically employed to identify objects once they had been spotted. They would not have been used to help spot icebergs. However, there was no moon and the sea was flat calm, making iceberg detection more difficult. When an iceberg was eventually spotted directly in the ship's path just before 11:40 p.m., she was simply too close to avoid a collision.

Following the impact, the question immediately arose: how badly was the ship damaged? Initial reports seemed tentatively positive, but bad news was not long in coming. It was clear that the ship had sustained serious damage. To his credit, Captain Smith did not laxly put his trust in the concept of the 'unsinkable ship'. Instead, he ordered the ship's lifeboats uncovered and prepared, and then set off with one of the ship's chief designers, Thomas Andrews, to see personally how bad things really were. In the course of their inspection, things seemed serious, but it appears that there was still some reason for optimism when Captain Smith headed topside. Andrews continued his investigation, however, and soon found something horrible. He was seen racing topside, ashen, to inform the Captain that the *Titanic* would founder within an hour to an hour and a half. The ship had sustained intermittent damage along nearly a third of her starboard side. Her advanced system of watertight subdivision was rendered all but useless. From that point forward, it was a race against time, and it was not going to go well.

Because there were not enough lifeboats for all aboard, the news had to be handled carefully so as to prevent panic. As a result, many went uninformed of the ship's impending fate, even among the officer corps. The ship's band was sent to play and calm the nerves of passengers who were suddenly unsure of what exactly was going on around them. The ship still seemed safe to many, and as a result the officers initially got few volunteers and the first boats to leave were far from full. This further reduced an already insufficient lifeboat capacity, but it was vitally important to launch the boats quickly. As the ship's bow settled deeper and deeper into the sea, word came in that a single ship, the intermediate-sized Cunarder *Carpathia*, was coming to render assistance, but she was some four hours away. Another ship, visible on the horizon, did not respond to wireless messages or to the firing of distress rockets, seemingly oblivious to *Titanic*'s plight.

Fast though the disaster played out, there was still enough time for people to show great self-sacrifice and heroism. Where some officers maintained the 'women and children first' rule, many husbands sent their wives and families into the boats, then bravely stepped back and quietly awaited their own fates. Things were rather peaceful and orderly to begin with, but late in the disaster signs of chaos began to break forth; more people were willing to try to sneak into the lifeboats. Reports ran rife shortly after the disaster that in the last few minutes, officers had threatened to fire shots – or, some said, had actually done so – to keep order.

Time ran out before the final two collapsible lifeboats could even be launched, and they were floated from the deck. The ship's bow dived beneath the sea, and her stern reared up before the vessel split in half. The stern settled back before standing on end and sinking from sight at 2:20 a.m., two hours and forty minutes after the collision. Of the 2,208 aboard, 1,496 perished, including Captain Smith and Thomas Andrews. Only 712 survived.

The stunning news began to break the next day to an astounded public. White Star officials wept openly at their announcement of the loss of the

Perhaps the most famous public spaces aboard *Olympic* and *Titanic* were their first-class grand staircases. This illustration shows a woman descending the forward staircase.

liner and her precious human cargo. Although in subsequent years the loss of the *Titanic* would be credited with bringing an end to the age of confidence and optimism in human endeavour, in reality the close of that gilded age would only come two years later. Nevertheless, the disaster shook man's confidence in technology to its very core. If the largest and best-built ship in the world could sink in less than three hours after blundering across an iceberg, what else could happen?

Immediately after the *Titanic* disaster, extra lifeboats were brought aboard *Olympic* and other ships. This scene gives a unique idea of how things looked on *Titanic's* boat deck as the lifeboats were prepared for loading.

The disaster moved regulatory bodies finally to require that ships carry lifeboats for all of their passengers and crew, which was particularly important because the next three wonder ships that would enter service, a German trio of behemoths, were designed to carry well over five thousand passengers and crew each. The first of these was the Hamburg-Amerika liner *Imperator*, with a length of 909 feet – or 918 feet, 8 inches if you included the figurehead mounted at her prow during her first season's service – and measured at 52,117 tons. She entered service in June 1913. The second, named *Vaterland*, entered service the following May. She was 950 feet long, and came in at a whopping 54,282 tons.

Hamburg-Amerika, like White Star, was focusing on offering luxury of accommodation and grand scale. However, the new vessels were given turbine engines, like those fitted to the *Lusitania* and *Mauretania*. The *Vaterland* and her younger sister – slated to be named *Bismarck* when she was launched on 20 June 1914 – would prove to be exceptionally fast ships for their size and unprecedented bulk. The interior first-class spaces of the *Imperator* and *Vaterland* were extraordinary. Their primary lounges, termed 'social halls,' sported ceilings 20 feet high, and boasted over 4,200 square feet of floor space each; down below, their Pompeian swimming baths sported classical Roman themes and were two full decks in height – a great leap forward over the swimming baths installed on previous liners such as the *Adriatic*, *Olympic* and *Titanic*.

Meanwhile, Cunard had been following up on their sister speedsters with the construction of a third vessel, which was in the event named *Aquitania*. The *Aquitania* was 901 feet 6 inches in length, and bore a gross tonnage of 45,647. Built at the John Brown shipyards, where the *Lusitania* had been built, she was launched on 21 April 1913. During the following year, an elaborate scheme of decoration was fitted in the liner's first- and second-class spaces – so much

The behemoth Hamburg-Amerika liner *Imperator* of 1913 sported a tremendously tall trio of funnels. Although vast and luxurious, she was also notoriously top-heavy. Her funnels were quickly shortened as part of an effort to improve her stability.

so that she would earn the nickname 'The Ship Beautiful'. Although she would never compete for the Blue Riband, this four-funnelled vessel would become one of the most popular and long-lived of all Atlantic liners.

On 29 May 1914, just the day before the *Aquitania* was to begin her maiden voyage to New York, the Canadian Pacific liner *Empress of Ireland* was leaving Canada bound for Liverpool. While navigating the St Lawrence River near Rimouski, she was enveloped in a thick fogbank. The Norwegian collier *Storstad* was also in the area. Through a series of questionable decisions made by the officers on the bridges of both ships, the *Storstad* ended up ramming the *Empress of Ireland* just before 2:00 a.m. The prestigious liner quickly lost power and began to sag onto her damaged starboard side. The list rendered many of her lifeboats unlaunchable, thus negating the usefulness of post-*Titanic* regulation improvements. She was carrying some 1,477 passengers and crew at the time. As it was the first night after leaving port, most of the passengers were thoroughly unfamiliar with the ship's layout; the darkness and the ship's list only worsened their disorientation. When the *Empress of Ireland* sank, some fourteen minutes after the collision, some 1,012 died. There had been no time for heroics, like those on the *Titanic* two years before. In the raw struggle for survival, roughly 60 per cent of the crew had survived simply because they were familiar with the ship's layout, while only 18 per cent of the third-class passengers survived. Many of those who perished never made it out of the ship's interior spaces, and were left to suffer a ghastly death in smothering blackness. It was a horrific end to an otherwise prestigious career, and news of the sinking cast a pall over the *Aquitania*'s maiden voyage, which began on 30 May.

Meanwhile, the White Star Line was attempting to pull itself together in the wake of its own *Titanic* tragedy. In November 1911, Harland & Wolff had begun construction on a third liner of the *Olympic*-class, which was eventually named *Britannic*. Her construction was in its earliest stages when *Titanic* slid beneath the cold waters of the North Atlantic. Thus many of the alterations and improvements required – and which were so difficult to implement on *Olympic* – could be made on paper. When the *Britannic* was launched, she was called 'one of the most daring examples of modern marine engineering'. Her watertight integrity had been significantly upgraded over that of the *Titanic*, and she was designed to carry more than enough lifeboats for all of her passengers and crew. In the most unusual lifeboat storage and launching idea ever to grace the North Atlantic, these craft were to be stowed under enormous gantry davits. The davits were so large that they would be obvious from virtually any angle, but that was really the point – not only would the gantry davits launch the lifeboats quickly in an emergency, but they were also a highly visible sign of White Star's commitment to safety, a tremendous reassurance to a jittery travelling public.

At the time of the 882-foot 9-inch *Britannic*'s launch on 26 February 1914, it was said that 'such triumphs of industry and highly developed skill prove that the world is not going backward, but that we are moving forward with longer strides than were ever before attempted. All such examples are true harbingers of "peace on earth, good will to men".' Unfortunately, peace was about to be taken from the earth as it never had been before.

A finely detailed portrait of Cunard's *Aquitania* entering New York harbour, c. 1914.

CUNARD LINE

R.M.S. AQUITANIA.

A CALL TO ARMS

THE GREAT WAR – or as it was later known, the First World War – erupted on the world scene in the summer of 1914. The *Aquitania* was quickly converted into an armed auxiliary for the Royal Navy. The *Olympic* diverted from New York to Halifax, blacking out her lights and dashing to safety at a remarkable speed of over 25 knots. The German liner *Vaterland* was caught at her North River pier in Hoboken, just across from Manhattan. She would remain there for three years. The other German giant, *Imperator*, was kept safely tucked away on the River Elbe in Germany. Liners like the *Lusitania*, *Mauretania* and *Olympic* were busily engaged through the early months of autumn in bringing neutral Americans home from a war-torn Europe. Once their task had been completed, however, passenger traffic on the Atlantic began to decline sharply. German vessels began to mine the traffic lanes around the British Isles, and German U-boats began to prowl the waters looking for victims. With little revenue-earning traffic and dangers mounting, the *Mauretania* and *Olympic* were withdrawn from service and laid up. *Aquitania* was idled as well, after suffering a collision with Leyland liner *Canadian*. Soon, only the *Lusitania* remained in service among the first-rate transatlantic liners.

On 1 May 1915, the famous Cunarder departed New York on the return leg of her 101st round-trip voyage. She had aboard 1,959 passengers and crew, many of them neutral Americans. The eastbound crossing was more or less ideal; however, on the evening of 6 May, the Admiralty began to broadcast wireless messages warning her Captain, William Turner, that there was danger from German submarines in the waters ahead. As the liner closed on the Irish coast early the next afternoon, the sun was shining brightly and threats from enemy submarines must have seemed distant. Then, without warning, the German submarine *U-20* sent a single torpedo into the *Lusitania*'s starboard side. A second explosion quickly followed. The ship heeled over onto her wounded side and began to sink by the bow. Confusion and pandemonium reigned. Attempts to launch the lifeboats were complicated by the list. The ship sank in an astounding eighteen minutes.

Opposite:
This rare view looks down from the aft funnel of United States Troop Transport #1326: USS *Leviathan*. Originally the *Vaterland* of 1914, she was commandeered by the Americans when they entered the war.

Above: Passengers lounge on the deck of White Star's *Adriatic* on 23 August 1914, about three weeks after the war began. *Adriatic* later served as a troopship, survived the war, and was eventually scrapped in 1935.

A total of 1,198 men, women and children died; the concept that civilians could remain untouched in this new breed of 'world war' was shattered. The loss of American neutrals in the disaster set relations between America and the Germans on edge. It was not, however, the flashpoint that sent America into the fray; that would not come for another two years. The sinking was the third in a series of appalling maritime catastrophes that had taken place within a mere three years.

Soon the other Atlantic liners would face great dangers. The *Mauretania* and *Aquitania* were quickly pressed into service as troopships and began bringing thousands of troops to the fronts in the Mediterranean theatre of operations. During the course of this engagement, the *Mauretania* was attacked without warning and only just managed to avoid being struck by a torpedo.

During the autumn of 1915, there was a great need to bring wounded soldiers home from the fronts. *Mauretania* and *Aquitania* were both transformed into hospital ships. The unfinished *Britannic* was requisitioned in November 1915 for the same task. Her interior spaces were almost completely unfinished, and that allowed an easy conversion for her new assignment. Outside, her hull was painted white, and her four funnels were given a thorough dousing of mustard-yellow paint. A broad green stripe encircled her hull, interspersed occasionally with red crosses. This was the typical hospital ship colour scheme, but it was certainly quite different from that she would have sported as a White Star liner. She joined the *Mauretania* and *Aquitania* in late December 1915, but with the evacuation of Gallipoli that same month, the need for hospital ships soon began to decline. By the late winter of 1915–16, the three giant ships were laid up again, awaiting a decision regarding their

future use. On 1 March, the *Mauretania* was released, and the *Aquitania* was returned to Cunard on 10 March. The company was given £150,000 to spend restoring the two ships to their pre-war splendour. The *Britannic* was laid up from 11 April to 6 June at half rate, but was finally released as well. She was returned to White Star along with £76,000 to refit her for commercial service.

Work on restoring these ships continued into the summer, but then the Mediterranean theatre heated up once more, and the need for hospital ships arose again. On 21 July, the *Aquitania* was again requisitioned and transformed back into a hospital ship; the *Britannic* was called up on 28 August. The *Mauretania* never did become a hospital ship again; she instead made two voyages to Halifax in the autumn of 1916 to bring troops out to Europe. During those two voyages, she supplemented the *Olympic*, which was engaged on the Halifax run as a troopship from March 1916 to December 1917. The *Mauretania* did not remain in service with the *Olympic* however, and was laid up throughout all of 1917. Meanwhile, the *Aquitania* and *Britannic* had continued their voyages of mercy to the Mediterranean.

Although hospital ships were supposed to be protected under the rules of the Geneva Convention, paper treaties did not eliminate the dangers posed by indiscriminate mines. While in the Kea Channel in the Aegean Sea, on the morning of 21 November 1916, the *Britannic* struck a single mine. One Voluntary Aid Detachment nurse, Winifred Greenwood, remembered the explosion as 'a terrific crash [which] shook the ship from end to end'. All of the crockery and dishes at the breakfast tables shook and rattled in response. Although the damage should have been confined to the ship's forward areas, many watertight doors were open at the time, and flooding quickly taxed the limit of *Britannic*'s advanced safety features. When open portholes near the

Above: Third of the *Olympic*-class liners, *Britannic* was requisitioned for use as a hospital ship during the war. Sunk by a mine, and largely forgotten for the next eighty years, she remains the largest wreck on the seafloor. (IWM HU 090768)

Opposite bottom: A rare photo of the *Mauretania* (*left*) and *Aquitania* (*right*) together while both were serving as troopships during the Dardanelles Expedition.

An artist's view of the troopship *Aquitania* steaming through heavy seas. While she rides more or less comfortably, one of her smaller escorts pluckily dashes through a wave.

waterline began to submerge, they admitted a deadly influx of seawater, and overwhelmed her watertight subdivision completely. Her Captain, Charles Bartlett, tried to beach the ship. Meanwhile, preparations for evacuation were made. Unfortunately, two boats were launched prematurely, and were drawn into the still-churning propellers, creating a devastating scene of human carnage. The *Britannic* succumbed to her wounds fifty-five minutes after the single explosion. Of the 1,062 personnel who had been aboard, only thirty were lost. Captain Bartlett stepped from the bridge wing as she sank from under his feet and both he and Nurse Greenwood survived the sinking.

The *Aquitania* was laid up for almost the entirety of 1917, but changes were in the air once more. On 2 April 1917, the diplomatic breach between the United States and Germany reached breaking point. On that day, President Wilson addressed the US Congress and asked for a formal declaration of war.

On the night of 5–6 April 1917, hours before America formally entered the conflict, a group of determined US Government officials swarmed over the German liners laid up on the New Jersey waterfront; the greatest prize among these was the German liner *Vaterland*, still the largest complete ship in the world at the time. Her name was formally changed to *Leviathan* at the suggestion of President Wilson himself, and over the next seven months the liner was transformed into the world's largest troopship. Her capacity was, astoundingly, over 14,000 troops.

Eventually, during 1918, most of the surviving great liners came together in service on the Atlantic as troopships – *Olympic*, *Aquitania*, *Mauretania* and *Leviathan*. Throughout the year they carried tens of thousands of fresh troops out to the long-stalemated battlefronts. Soon, this surge of troops had overwhelmed the Central Powers. On 11 November 1918, the war that forever changed the world ended. Throughout the remainder of 1918 and much of 1919, the liners – now joined by the *Imperator*, which had been commandeered on the River Elbe – turned the flow in the opposite direction. They returned hundreds of thousands of American and Canadian troops back to their homes to be reunited with their families.

Once their call to arms was complete and the ships had been returned to their owners, they were all sent to various shipyards for thorough overhauls. Their grime and wartime fittings removed and their splendid interiors restored to their proper places, they were then prepared to return to their originally intended roles as luxury liners. The question was: how would the great liners adapt to a new and thoroughly different world?

An aerial photo of the *Olympic* packed with troops and the extra lifeboats to carry them in the event of an emergency.

Mauretania entering New York harbour on 2 December 1918, just after the Armistice. With the war over, happy troops celebrate their homecoming. Everyone looked forward to a respite from years of bitter worldwide warfare.

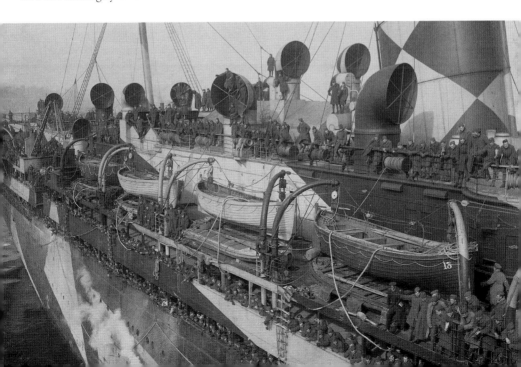

PEACE AND A NEW GENERATION

IT MIGHT have seemed, as the 1920s began, as if things were going to return to a pre-war 'normal' for the transatlantic liners. However, changes were on the horizon. In the first place, the crack liners, gleaming in their pre-war company colours again, had been converted to burn oil rather than coal, as oil enjoyed many advantages. Stokehold crews could be reduced by 75 per cent or more; while thousands of suddenly unemployed coal stokers may have groused about the change, the hellish conditions formerly suffered by the remaining stokers were improved dramatically. Refuelling in port was also made much simpler and cleaner, and could be accomplished in much less time than with coal.

Even as demand for passenger travel burgeoned, there came the question of what to do with the former German merchant marine, which had been seized by the victorious Allies as war reparations. Eventually, White Star purchased the unfinished *Bismarck* and she was completed in Germany to their specifications. She entered service with them in 1922 as the *Majestic*. At 956 feet in length and with a gross tonnage of 56,551, she was clearly the world's largest ship. They also purchased another ex-German liner, the *Columbus*, and she entered service as the *Homeric*. When the *Homeric* was paired with the *Olympic*, White Star had what was, in the end, a very popular and successful set of liners with which to carry on their weekly passenger service throughout the decade. Cunard purchased the former *Imperator*, turning her into their great *Berengaria* and sending her into service with the *Mauretania* and *Aquitania*.

The United States took the *Leviathan* and sent William Francis Gibbs – who would go on to become one of America's foremost naval architects – and a team of men to go over the ship with a fine-tooth comb. Every inch of her old wiring was removed and replaced with wiring of superior quality. She received many other upgrades and improvements, until she emerged in the summer of 1923 as one of the finest ocean liners on the Atlantic. Gibbs had even re-measured the ship's gross tonnage, utilising every loophole in the American measuring system, until she had reached 59,957 tons.

Opposite:
A beautiful piece of artwork from *L'Illustration* depicting the *Normandie*'s first-class dining room populated by elegant passengers.

White Star's *Majestic*, the world's largest ship until the introduction of the *Normandie*. Originally launched as the German liner *Bismarck*, third of the *Imperator*-class trio, her completion had ground to a halt during the war.

Another ex-German liner which saw service with White Star was the *Homeric*. Although smaller than *Olympic* and *Majestic*, she was a fine and comfortable ship and saw service well into the 1930s.

The Americans, running the ship under the banner of the United States Lines, were quick to stir up controversy with this measurement by calling her the world's largest ship. For those who really knew the whole truth, however, the *Majestic* never lost the official title – even if it was hotly debated by those with a vested interest throughout the remainder of the decade.

Just as the great liners were coming back into service and settling back down to their routines,

A wine bill from the *Homeric* dated 10 April 1925. The total was given in British and American currency, and could be paid in whichever of the two was more convenient.

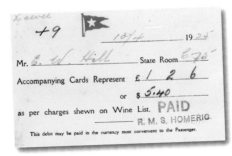

This photograph was taken on the trial trip of the *Leviathan*, just after her extensive conversion for service as an American passenger liner. Captain Herbert Hartley directs the attention of naval architect William Francis Gibbs to something on the horizon.

there came another significant change. This happened when the United States began to restrict the inflow of immigrants to their shores to a mere fraction of what it had been before the war. This was a major change for steamship companies because previously a good deal of their profit margins had come from carrying thousands of immigrants in basic accommodation to the 'New World'. With this flow cut dramatically, the steamship companies introduced 'tourist' class accommodation. This new class was designed to offer inexpensive accommodation to tourists headed to Europe, thus bolstering the companies' profit margins. The British liners enjoyed an advantage in offering such services, since many Americans suffering from the effects of Prohibition looked forward to being able to enjoy the alcohol that these still carried.

With people looking to forget the horrors of the Great War, and with unprecedented financial prosperity in the world, business boomed throughout the 1920s for the liners. In many ways, things felt much as they had been before the war, but there were also changes. The social customs and even social barriers were a little more relaxed. The clientele was also changing. The new elite of first class were the film stars of Hollywood – Douglas Fairbanks, Mary Pickford and many others. Jazz replaced ragtime in the repertoires of ship's bands, passengers merrily danced the Charleston and the Turkey Trot in the ballrooms and at times even along the open decks, and it seemed that the good times would go on forever.

This September 1920 view shows second- and third-class passengers enjoying moderate weather on the stern decks of the *Olympic*.

A new generation of liners began to enter service as the decade continued. The French Line's *Paris* entered service in 1921; she had been laid down in 1913 but her completion had been delayed by the war. Some 764 feet in length and of 34,569 tons, the *Paris* was not wholly remarkable externally, with three closely spaced funnels. Internally, however, she was stunning, with an eclectic but effective mix of traditional interior design and more modern themes. When she entered service, she was the largest French merchant vessel in operation. In 1926, she was joined by a noteworthy running mate, the *Ile de France*. This new vessel was somewhat larger than

The French liner *Paris* entering New York, probably at the end of her maiden voyage.

Above:
The *Ile de France* of 1927. Looking at her from the outside, no one could have guessed at her revolutionary interior decoration.

Left:
The first-class dining room of the *Ile de France* shows a forward-looking scheme of décor. Previous ships had looked to the past for inspiration, but that trend was ending.

The breathtaking first-class staircase and foyer of the *Ile de France*.

the *Paris*, at 43,153 tons, and she turned the shipping industry on its head with her bold Art Deco interiors. In a single instant, all of the pre-war vessels began to look dated; they were clearly from another era.

Then the Germans re-appeared on the Atlantic with their squat speedsters *Bremen* and *Europa*. The *Bremen*, 938 feet long and of 51,656 tons, made her maiden voyage in July 1929. She instantly took the Blue Riband from the venerable but aging *Mauretania*. The slightly smaller *Europa* followed in March 1930. In 1932, the Italian Line

Return of the Germans: squat but speedy *Europa* leaves port to begin her career.

entered the fray with their 51,062-ton speedster *Rex*. This vessel took the Blue Riband from the *Bremen* and *Europa*, and she was soon joined by the slightly smaller, slightly slower but magnificently appointed *Conte di Savoia*.

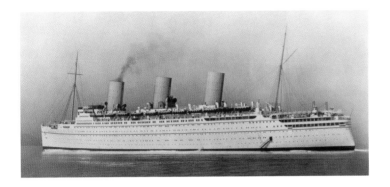

The *Empress of Britain*, successor to the 1906 ship of the same name. Built by the same yard that constructed *Lusitania*, *Aquitania* and *Queen Mary*, the *Empress of Britain* was a splendid, and often overlooked, liner of the 1930s.

At the same time, the Canadian Pacific Railway commissioned their second *Empress of Britain*. Entering service in 1931, she was 760 feet long and had a gross tonnage of 42,500.

Meanwhile, the 'Roaring Twenties' had come to a sudden end with the crash of the American stock market and the onset of the Great Depression in late 1929. Fewer people had the wherewithal to spend money on unnecessary travel; steamship lines' ledgers quickly slid from the black to the red. During the off-season, many of the liners supplemented crossings with cheap 'booze cruises', many of these made to tropical waters. Yet it was clear that many of the pre-war giants were beginning to show their age. Their decoration looked to the past, not the future. More passengers were

A 1936–8 view of prestigious liners docked in New York. From top to bottom: *Europa*, *Rex*, *Normandie*, White Star's motor ship *Georgic*, and *Berengaria*.

Above: *Mauretania*'s hull was painted white in May of 1933. This stern view was taken during her 5–18 August 1933 cruise to the West Indies.

Above: Passengers enjoy the sea air on *Mauretania*'s 23 March–2 April 1934 cruise to the West Indies.

demanding private bathrooms, something that was rather rare on the Atlantic before the war. While cruising in the heat of the tropics, many liners did not even have swimming pools. Cunard's *Mauretania*, her hull painted white in her later years, was such a case, and her crew was forced to improvise with temporary canvas pools. None of those liners were graced with the luxury of true 'air conditioning', and their passengers frequently sweltered in stifling summer or, during cruises, tropical heat. They were clearly from another time, a different world, and they were far older than their years suggested. To remain competitive, both Cunard and White Star saw the need to best

Right: Passengers find relief from oppressive tropical heat in one of the *Mauretania*'s two canvas-and-wood swimming pools. This particular West Indies cruise during July 1932 encompassed 4,908 miles while carrying 720 passengers.

both the new German liners and the forthcoming Italian ships; they began to move forward with plans for the next generation of ultra-large, ultra-fast ships.

Harland & Wolff commenced construction of White Star's new vessel, to be named *Oceanic*. John Brown & Company began construction on Cunard's ship, which would eventually be named *Queen Mary*. Meanwhile, the French Line had started work on its own contender in this challenge, which would be named *Normandie*. Because of the effects of the Depression, all three companies ran out of money and had to approach their respective governments for financial aid. Britain agreed to subsidies only if Cunard and White Star merged. The two rival lines agreed, becoming the amalgamated Cunard-White Star Line on 10 May 1934. The *Oceanic* was sacrificed on the Belfast shipyard's ways so that work on the *Queen Mary* could proceed. The French Line also found themselves in dire financial straits, but after they obtained a loan from the French Government work on their vessel continued, as well. The race for the trophy would be between the *Queen Mary* and the *Normandie*.

During the height of the Depression, most of the older ships went to the breakers, *Olympic*, *Mauretania*, *Berengaria*, *Leviathan* and *Majestic* among them.

The hull of the *Queen Mary* takes shape at the John Brown shipyards in Scotland, shortly before her launch.

The *Queen Mary* during her fitting-out in Scotland. Her masts are in place, as well as her forward two funnels. However the aft funnel is still under construction, and no lifeboats have yet been fitted.

41

This colourful view shows the *Queen Mary*'s garden lounge.

The completed *Queen Mary* at anchor. Her profile was at once stately, proud, stodgy and outdated – an overgrown *Mauretania* or *Aquitania*.

The old *Paris* burned at Le Havre on 18 April 1939 and was a total loss. The *Aquitania* was still in service, but she was aging and her days were clearly numbered. It seemed that the future lay entirely with the latest generation of liners, and in the great record-breakers soon to come.

The *Queen Mary* and *Normandie* could hardly have been more similar, or yet, more diametrically opposed. Although they were roughly the same size (just over 1,000 feet long, of about 80,000 tons each, and each sporting three enormous smokestacks) the *Normandie* was built to cater for its first-class passengers – the likes of Ginger Rogers and Fred Astaire. The *Queen Mary*, on

Despite her exterior restraint, the *Queen Mary* proved the most popular ship on the Atlantic when she entered service. Here passengers gather for a concert in the first-class lounge during one of her earliest crossings.

the other hand, would be built to attract great numbers of tourist-class passengers. The *Normandie*'s hull form was revolutionary, proposed by Russian engineer Vladimir Yourkevitch; Cunard studied Yourkevitch's hull design, but believed that its advantages would lie only in very calm seas, which were quite rare on the North Atlantic. They thus built a very traditional hull for the great speedster. The *Queen Mary* also sported a traditional powerplant, whereas the *Normandie* was given a revolutionary turbo-electric plant, with steam creating electricity to drive her propellers. However, the *Queen Mary*'s direct-drive turbines would give her much more power to attain high speed than that available to the French ship. The *Normandie*'s interior first-class spaces were awe-inspiring Art Deco cathedrals, while the *Queen Mary*'s were far more restrained. It was said that on the *Queen Mary* the 'modern influence undoubtedly exists, but rampant modernity has been studiously and successfully avoided'.

A 1936 or later photo of the *Normandie*. Her profile was clean, dramatic and revolutionary.

A very rare artistic rendering, taken from a cigarette card, of the *Normandie*'s bridge.

An artist's take on the scene as one of *Normandie*'s engineers monitors the activity of the vessel's revolutionary powerplant.

Passengers toss rings and play shuffleboard atop the *Normandie*'s tourist-class lounge in this post-1936 view.

The *Normandie* entered service first, on 29 May 1935. She was 1,029 feet 4 inches in length, and was initially measured at 79,280 tons. On her maiden voyage, she took the Blue Riband with an average speed of 29.98 knots – even achieving 31.69 knots at one point. This record was despite having encountered some periods of moderately rough weather. She was also very stable in poor weather; when she rolled, she was quick to return to the vertical, earning a reputation as a 'snappy-roller' and giving her passengers a spirited ride.

The *Queen Mary* entered service on 27 May 1936. She was 1,019 feet 6 inches long, but was initially registered at 80,774 tons – slightly larger than the *Normandie*. Although she did not take the Blue Riband on her maiden voyage, she did so that August. She also consistently carried far more passengers than the *Normandie*, but she was a very poor roller at sea, drunkenly sagging to one side or the other and only reluctantly returning to vertical. Rivalry between the French and British ships was keen. Both ships were re-measured to take the prize as 'world's largest ship' through the rest of the 1930s.

Cunard then proceeded with a sister for the *Queen Mary*, named *Queen Elizabeth*. She would be longer than her sister and the *Normandie*, at 1,031 feet and 83,673 tons. She would never see service against the French liner, however, for the world was about to plunge into a second, and far more devastating, world war.

This view, from 1936 or later, shows passengers shooting clay pigeons from the *Normandie*'s port stern sections.

45

RETURN TO CONFLICT

O N 1 September 1939 Germany invaded Poland, and the Second World War began. The rival *Queen Mary* and *Normandie* were both caught in New York, and remained safely in the neutral port as hostilities commenced. The old *Aquitania* was eastbound for England in commercial service, but managed to avoid encounters with Hitler's already-active U-boats. She was called into government service as a troop transport by November. The unfinished *Queen Elizabeth* was a prime target for German bombers, so she made a nail-biting dash from Scotland to New York in early 1940. For two weeks, the three largest ships in the world – *Normandie*, *Queen Mary* and *Queen Elizabeth* – were side by side in Manhattan. Then the *Queen Mary* departed, entering service as a troopship. The *Queen Elizabeth* was next, and soon the *Normandie* sat alone, her future uncertain. Britain was quick to use its merchant fleet to move men from the corners of the Empire to the fronts. Ships like the *Queens* found themselves running tens of thousands of troops from Australia.

Whatever route they plied, much of the story was the same. During the conversion process, most of the ships' interior fittings were stripped down to the bare minimum. Racks of temporary bunks allowed troops to be squeezed in like sardines. The carrying capacity of the *Queen Mary* and *Queen Elizabeth* skyrocketed to approximately sixteen thousand men each. Masses of young troops forged up the gangplanks and boarded the ships on sailing day. Once they had arrived in their quarters, by and large they stayed put so that they did not get underfoot. Meals were served in shifts; sometimes, men were allowed up on the decks to enjoy good weather or to participate in physical training classes. Meanwhile, the ships themselves faced dangers from enemy submarines and aeroplanes. Although travelling at high speed, the ships routinely changed course in a pattern called 'zig-zagging', in order to present a more difficult target. This lengthened the time it took to make the voyage. However, by the time troops reached the fronts they seemed ready and eager to face the Axis powers.

For over two years, this routine dragged on. Then, on 7 December 1941, Japan attacked the American fleet at Pearl Harbor, Hawaii, plunging the US

Opposite:
The *Queen Mary*
after conversion
from luxury liner
to troopship.
Troops festoon
her open decks;
the two *Queens*
moved so many
troops that
Churchill credited
them with
shortening the war
by a year.

A pair of ladies standing on the *Normandie*'s sun deck in September 1939. The ship was then laid up at her New York pier, never to make another crossing.

After eighteen months of salvage work, which necessitated the removal of her upper works, the *Lafayette*, formerly the *Normandie*, was righted, but she was later scrapped. The French Government was given $13.5 million in recompense for her loss, with the understanding that the money would be used to buy US-built Liberty ships.

into the conflict. Before the month was out, the *Normandie* was seized and work began to convert her into a troopship, renamed USS *Lafayette*. Workers descended upon her stately interiors and began removing them for storage. On 9 February 1942, this process resulted in an outbreak of fire. Much of the ship's superstructure was consumed, and fireboats eagerly doused her in water. The fires were put out, but the damage was done and the accumulated water caused the *Normandie* to roll onto her side in defeat. Although she was refloated, by that time the war was progressing so well for the Allies that there was no foreseeable use for her, and she was ignominiously scrapped.

The *Queen Mary* herself was the subject of a sad incident on 2 October 1942. After crossing the Atlantic bound for Scotland without escort, the great liner was entering the range of the Luftwaffe. The HMS *Curacoa*, an anti-aircraft light cruiser, and six destroyers met the liner to provide air and submarine defence. The group began carefully choreographed zig-zag manoeuvres, but somehow the *Curacoa* managed to end up directly in front of the *Queen Mary*'s prow. The cruiser was struck, sliced clean in half, and sank almost immediately. The *Queen Mary* – with over 10,000 troops aboard – was unable to render assistance for fear of enemy attack. Some 329 sailors aboard the *Curacoa* were killed, and the *Queen Mary* required repairs to the damage her bows had sustained.

Many other great ships suffered worse, and were lost in the conflict, including the *Rex*, *Conte di Savoia*, *Bremen* and *Empress of Britain*. This fate befell the German *Wilhelm Gustloff*, a rather small 25,484-ton cruise ship. She was

torpedoed on 30 January 1945 while evacuating troops and civilians from Kiel. About 10,600 souls were on board at the time of her loss, and of these it is likely that around 9,400 perished. This ghastly toll of human carnage thus stands – probably forever – as the worst catastrophe in maritime history.

Fortunately, things went far better for both British *Queens* and the *Aquitania*. All three emerged from the war more or less unscathed, although certainly well worn from their exertions and with a number of close calls under their collective belts. The *Europa* also survived the conflict. The *Ile de France* – which had been commandeered and turned into a British troopship – emerged unscathed as well. As guns around the world went silent in 1945, and rubble-strewn nations tried to piece themselves back together, the Atlantic liners also stepped bravely into the future.

On 11 July 1945, the *Queen Mary* arrives in New York. The troops celebrate enthusiastically, and they are heartily greeted by many female Red Cross workers.

The *Aquitania*, the only great liner to serve in both world wars, departs from Southampton, seen off by a small crowd.

Getting there **is half the** *fun!*

The experienced traveler knows what the new traveler discovers with delight: an ocean voyage is the gayest, most relaxing holiday in the world . . . especially aboard a Cunarder! So when you go to Europe . . . whether for business or fun . . . don't miss the sheer joy of a Cunard crossing . . . the brilliant round of activities, the high-spirited companionship, the spacious luxury, the glorious tonic of the clean salt air . . . and a gourmet's choice of delicacies to satisfy your sharpened appetite. This is the life you'll love!

YOUR TRAVEL AGENT WILL SERVE YOU AT NO EXTRA

No wonder more people prefer CUNARD

From New York: QUEEN ELIZABETH · QUEEN MARY · MAURETANIA · CARONIA · BRITANNIC · MEDIA · PARTHIA

UNCERTAIN FUTURE

Shortly after hostilities ceased, on 16 October 1946, the *Queen Elizabeth* made her maiden voyage as a passenger ship. After an extensive refit, the *Queen Mary* returned to the Atlantic in her Cunard livery in July 1947. Two years later, the beloved *Ile de France* – stripped of her third funnel but restored to her former glory – returned to service with the French Line. The former German liner *Europa* was handed over to the French, and, after a complicated overhaul, entered service with the *Ile de France* as the *Liberté* in 1950.

Passenger traffic on the North Atlantic was again booming, and there was great optimism in shipping circles. Even as the great old Cunarder *Aquitania* – a veteran of both world wars, and with nearly thirty-six years of service to her credit – was sold off to the breakers, a new generation of liners was being constructed.

Perhaps the most startling of these began its maiden voyage in July 1952. At 990 feet in length, and of some 53,330 tons, the American superliner *United States* did not threaten to take the record as the world's largest or longest liner. What she did sport was an ultra-modern hull – 'sleek as a shark' – and a revolutionary powerplant with nearly a quarter of a million horsepower at its disposal. On her trials, she had reached 38.32 knots while putting some 241,785 shaft horsepower into the sea. She was the new flagship of the United States Lines, and had been designed by legendary naval architect William Francis Gibbs. On her maiden eastbound voyage, she took the Blue Riband from the *Queen Mary* at an average speed of 35.59 knots, and raised the westbound record on her return to 34.51 knots. She was a highly successful passenger-carrying liner, and an extremely safe one as well. Gibbs' penchant for fire prevention meant that the only wood in the entire ship was found in the butcher's block, the piano and the bilge keels alongside the hull. Despite her great success in terms of the number of bookings, some passengers preferred the feel of the old pre-war *America* because of her somewhat more charming interior décor. Nevertheless, the *United States* was – and remains – the fastest ocean liner in the world, and had a very special charm.

Opposite:
A 1950s Cunard advertisement – featuring the *Queen Mary* proudly at the top – proclaims that 'Getting there is half the fun!'

The Italians burst back onto the scene in 1953 with their new *Andrea Doria*, which was followed in 1954 by a nearly identical sister, the *Cristoforo Columbo*. Both ships were rather small, at only 700 feet and 29,000 tons each, but they were enormously popular and well-travelled. On the night of 25 July 1956, however, the splendid *Andrea Doria* was struck by the Swedish ship *Stockholm* in a fogbank south of Nantucket. Some 46 people aboard the Italian liner and five aboard the Swedish ship were killed in the collision. The *Andrea Doria* listed over onto her starboard side and began to sink, albeit very slowly thanks to her watertight subdivision. Radioed distress calls brought the

The post-war *Ile de France* emerged from an extensive overhaul with two rather than three funnels.

From 1952 on, the SS *United States* has held the title of 'world's fastest ocean liner'.

assistance of several vessels, including the *Ile de France*, and the remainder of the *Andrea Doria*'s passengers and crew were rescued. Then, about eleven hours after the collision, the liner succumbed to her wounds and sank. In rather a novel twist of maritime catastrophes, a film crew was able to record her last minutes of life from the air as they flew overhead.

The loss of the *Andrea Doria* was a blow to the shipbuilding industry, but worse was to follow. Jet aeroplane transportation had steadily been making inroads into the passenger lists of the liners; in 1957 more chose to take passage by air than by sea for the first time in history, and the revenue continued to decline. In 1959, the aging *Ile de France* was sold to Japanese shipbreakers. In a last turn, she starred in the MGM film *The Last Voyage*.

The North Atlantic puts every ship, no matter how large or fast, to the test. Here the *United States* battles a gale in May 1966.

Passengers on the Italian liner *Andrea Doria* converse with each other and with one of the ship's officers.

She – ironically – played an aging liner about to be broken up, which sank on her final trip. The ship was used for the filming of most of the movie, and was actually sunk on a sandbar to portray the fictional liner's end. She was later refloated and scrapped.

Even as air transportation ascended to first place on the North Atlantic, two last, great Atlantic liners from that generation were already in the works. For the French Line, their next monster – appropriately named *France* – was laid down on 7 October 1957 and she made her maiden voyage to New York in February 1962. The *France* was 1,035 feet 8 inches in length, with a gross tonnage of 66,348. She was also quite swift, attaining 35.21 knots during her trials and with a service speed of about 31 knots.

The final minutes of the *Andrea Doria* as the dying liner rolls onto her starboard side.

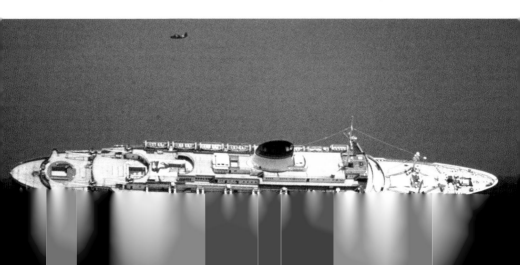

A staged promotional photograph showing the comfort of tourist-class accommodation aboard the *France*. A friendly bellboy presents 'passengers' with a *bon voyage* gift.

The *France* – clearly a successor to the *Normandie* in hull form, if not funnel design – is nosed into her New York pier.

Meanwhile, Cunard was studying what sort of ship they might commission to replace their aging *Queens*. Their early interest was focused on a project called *Q3*; this would have proved highly unprofitable in the coming lean times, but fortunately for the line, it was never built. Finally, they settled on a design, the ship that would become known as *Queen Elizabeth 2*, or *QE2*. This vessel – some 963 feet long and of some 65,863 tons – started her trials

in November 1968, but encountered some significant technical problems. She did not make her maiden voyage until 2 May 1969, but on her trials she had managed to achieve some 32.66 knots for six hours. She broke with tradition in a number of respects, being custom-built to mix crossing and cruising; her single stovepipe funnel was a grey tube encased in a white airfoil, rather than Cunard's traditional orange-red. The *QE2* would become one of the greatest Atlantic liners of all time.

Meanwhile, in 1967 and 1968, the *Queen Mary* and *Queen Elizabeth* had been removed from service. The mighty *Queen Elizabeth* did not fare well, and ended up in

Models posing as passengers enjoy the *Queen Elizabeth*'s gymnasium, riding stationary bicycles and electric horses.

Dancing in the *Queen Mary*'s verandah grill. Again, the 'passengers' are very probably models in this publicity photo shoot.

A late 1971 photo shows the *Queen Elizabeth* in Hong Kong Harbour, being transformed into the *Seawise University*.

The *Seawise University* burning on 9 January 1972, almost certainly the victim of arson.

Hong Kong Harbour, purchased by a Taiwanese shipping tycoon named C.Y. Tung. Renamed *Seawise University*, she was undergoing renovations when she caught fire – apparently by arson – and burned at her mooring on 9 January 1972, a total loss. She was scrapped between 1974 and 1975, although some of her remains were left behind and remain on the bottom of the harbour to this day.

The *United States* was permanently laid up in November 1969, the victim not only of the popularity of air travel, but also of protracted labour disputes and strikes; the strikes had made her sailing schedule notoriously unreliable and, as a result, fewer passengers were willing to make bookings on her in later years.

Finally, the great *France* succumbed to the inevitable; by late 1974, oil prices were rising, labour disputes were growing in frequency and severity, and passenger numbers continued to dwindle. Then in September there came a four-week mutiny. When it ended, so did the *France*, and she was laid up.

The legendary lineage of the Atlantic liners had dwindled until only one ship, the *QE2*, carried the torch, criss-crossing the Atlantic in good weather and cruising in foul in a lonely vigil. It appeared that the great ships had come to an end. Or had they…?

The *Queen Elizabeth 2* in Liverpool in September 2007.

THE LEGENDS
LIVE ON

The *Queen Mary*'s orange-and-black trio of aluminium funnels – the slightly taller but badly rusted originals were replaced with look-alikes in 1968 – marches majestically aft from her bridge wing.

IN MAY 1980, a monstrous cruise ship entered service with Norwegian Cruise Lines. Named *Norway*, she was not, in fact, new. She was the *France*, under new ownership and thoroughly transformed for her new role as a Caribbean cruise liner. The cruise industry was just beginning to take off, and her eleventh-hour reprieve from the scrapyard was hailed as a triumph for maritime history. Indeed, that industry's growth has ensured that, at least in some form, the great ships live on.

The *Norway* – formerly the *France* – at St Thomas, US Virgin Islands, in the spring of 1996.

Two great vessels from the 'golden era' of the liners can be visited today. The *Queen Mary* rests quietly at Long Beach in California, a permanent floating hotel and tourist attraction. The SS *United States* has had an astonishing

60

series of escapes from the scrappers' torches through the years. Since 1996, she has been tied up in Philadelphia, Pennsylvania. Her exterior looks horribly shabby, but her engines are frequently 'turned over' and are reportedly in very good condition. Her future remains uncertain. Some of the wrecks of the great liners

The *Queen Mary's* bridge instruments still gleam invitingly, as if awaiting the command to take her back to sea.

remain and can also be seen today – these include the *Lusitania*, the *Britannic* and the *Andrea Doria*.

On 1 September 1985, the wreck of the *Titanic* was located, and public interest in that vessel and all historic liners was raised. On 19 December 1997, the most expensive movie made up to that time – James Cameron's epic *Titanic* – was released. The combination of a fictional romance and great attention to historic details left the world enthralled. As the film steamed on its way to becoming the largest-grossing movie in Hollywood industry, more and more people also began to take an interest in cruising.

Rusting and dilapidated, but not gone by any means, the legendary *United States* towers over her pier at Philadelphia in 2010.

The new form of the transatlantic liner: Cunard's *Queen Mary 2* makes her triumphant maiden voyage in 2004.

With the *QE2* aging, Cunard – by then owned by the Carnival Cruise Line – decided to build the largest transatlantic liner in history. Built in the same French shipyard that produced the *Normandie* and *France*, the *Queen Mary 2* was the next step forward in the evolution of the Atlantic liners. The 1,132-foot long 151,400-ton liner was the largest in history; her internal volume stands at over three times that of the *Titanic*. She made her maiden voyage on 12 January 2004, and is built to be equally comfortable crossing and cruising. With the retirement of the *QE2* in late 2008 – her own future as yet uncertain – the *Queen Mary 2* still sails the Atlantic, now paired up with two 90,000-ton running mates, *Queen Victoria* and *Queen Elizabeth*.

The *Norway* suffered a boiler explosion in 2003 and was subsequently scrapped. However, orders for immense cruise ships have proceeded. Carnival's rival Royal Caribbean placed into service three 154,000-ton vessels, followed by two of 220,000 tons each.

Throughout the twentieth century, the Atlantic liners evolved to meet new challenges and even took up cruising to supplement the profits of crossing the Atlantic. With great ships like the *Queen Mary 2* already several years into what promises to be a lengthy career, it seems that although times have changed, the great ships not only live on, but will continue to do so for some time.

FURTHER READING

Ardman, Harvey. *Normandie: Her Life and Times*. Franklin Watts, 1985.

Behe, George. *On Board R.M.S. Titanic – Memories of the Maiden Voyage*. Lulu Press, 2011.

Braynard, Frank O. and Westover, Robert Hudson. *SS United States: Fastest Ship in the World*. Turner Publishing, 2002.

Chirnside, Mark. *The Olympic-Class Ships*. The History Press, 2011.

Fitch, Tad, Layton, J. Kent, and Wormstedt, Bill. *On A Sea of Glass: The Life & Loss of the R.M.S. Titanic*. Amberley Publishing, 2011/2012.

Johnston, Ian. *Ships For A Nation: John Brown & Company, Clydebank*.

1847–1971. West Dumbartonshire Libraries & Museums, 2000.

Klistorner, Daniel and Hall, Steve (with Beveridge, Andrews, and Braunschweiger). *Titanic in Photographs*. The History Press, 2011.

Layton, J. Kent. *Lusitania: An Illustrated Biography*. Amberley Publishing, 2010.

Layton, J. Kent. *The Edwardian Superliners: A Trio of Trios*. Amberley Publishing, 2011.

Maxtone-Graham, John. *Queen Mary 2*. Bulfinch Press, 2004.

Maxtone-Graham, John. *France / Norway*. W. W. Norton, 2010.

Ocean Liner Virtual Museum (website): www.oceanlinermuseum.co.uk

Various contributors. *The Loss of the SS Titanic – A Centennial Reappraisal*. The History Press, 2011.

Zeni, David. *Forgotten Empress*. Halsgrove Publishing, 1998.

PLACES TO VISIT

UNITED KINGDOM

Brunel's SS Great Britain, Great Western Dockyard, Bristol BS1 6TY, UK.
Telephone: 0117 926 0680. Website: www.ssgreatbritain.org

Glasgow Riverside Museum, 100 Pointhouse Place, Glasgow, G3 8RS.
Telephone: 0141 287 2720. Website:
www.glasgowlife.org.uk/museums/our-museums/riverside-museum

Merseyside Maritime Museum, Albert Dock, Liverpool, L3 4AQ.
Telephone: 0151 478 4499. Website:
www.liverpoolmuseums.org.uk/maritime

Southampton Maritime Museum, The Wool House, Town Quay Road, SO14 2AR.
Telephone: 023 8022 3941. Website: www.southampton.gov.uk/
s-leisure/artsheritage/museums-galleries/maritimemuseum.aspx

Ulster Folk and Transport Museum, Cultra, Holywood, BT18 0EU.
Telephone: 028 9042 8428. Website: www.nmni.com/uftm

UNITED STATES

Hotel Queen Mary, 1126 Queens Highway, Long Beach, CA, US 90802.
Telephone: 001 877 342 0738. Website: www.queenmary.com

Mariners' Museum, 100 Museum Drive, Newport News, VA, US 23606.
Telephone: (001) 757 596 2222. Website: www.marinersmuseum.org

South Street Seaport Museum, 12 Fulton Street, New York City, NY, US 10038.
Telephone: (001) 212 748 8786. Website: www.seany.org

Titanic Branson, 3235 West 76 Country Boulevard, Branson, MO, US 65616.
Telephone: 001 800 381 7670. Website: www.titanicbranson.com

INDEX